Your Life is in Your Hands

FRAGILE

Handle with Care

C. Lisa Kendrick

Your Life is in Your Hands

FRAGILE

Handle with Care

C. Lisa Kendrick

YOUR LIFE IS IN YOUR HANDS

ISBN: 978-0-6151-6212-6

Teen & Young Adult Edition

Publisher: Kirsten Iman Publishing

Editor: SCM & Associates

Cover designed by: Success Unlimited Design Team

Website: www.leadtrainingsolutions.com

E-mails: ckendrick12@gmail.com
clk@leadtrainingsolutions.com

Printing in the United States of America

DEDICATION

To God, thanks for the gift. To Jesus, thanks for the lift.

To all who crossed my path and were able to leave an impression on my life, and left my world a little brighter.

ACKNOWLEDGEMENTS

To my circle of love ones for through the years they played an instrumental role in my journey of life. I am grateful for the good, the bad, and the ugly experiences. All of my life's episodes were addressed based on the experiences that I happily, and at times painfully, encountered in my world. I am appreciative for my learning process. Thanks to my friends who sat with me and listened to me as I transformed through this endeavor. Thanks for the constant encouragement. I would be remissed if I did not send thanks to my Kingdom family. Thanks to all who listened to and supported my desire to serve. God's grace is sufficient.

"For I know the plans I have for you," declared the Lord,

"plans to prosper you and not to harm you,

plans to give you hope and a future."

– Jeremiah 29:11

They will be like a well-watered garden

and they will sorrow no more.

– Jeremiah 31:12

AUTHOR'S NOTES

Life is fragile. We must handle our lives with care. This book has been in the making for many years and is long overdue. I give thanks for finally being graced with an open mind and clear vision. As I encountered more and more distressed youths, I truly began to hear the silent screams of their hearts. I have been blessed with the opportunity to speak to thousands of teenagers. Regardless of the city or state, I hear their shared cries as they yearn for someone to hear them and redirect their path.

I felt the dire need to carefully publish this book so you and I can put it in as many hands as possible. All of us need imparting into throughout life. As we grow, we desire some guidance and direction. We need a reminder that we are indeed important and necessary. Our future is bright and the dark stages in our lives are only to reveal the light in our journey. This book will unravel youths' and young adults' challenges and then walk them into their light.

It is time to renew the right spirit back into our future. It is time to help this estranged generation to come back into who they really are. It is time to educate our young adults on how they will overcome life's obstacles. This book is about putting our youths back on a positive path. This book was written to prepare it's readers to succeed in spite of life's hindrances. It was written for those who have encountered tough times in their lives. What you do from this point forward will make a difference. Stop reserving your positive mental and spiritual attitude and release your full potential.

CONTENTS

In the beginning...

Who Are You? 1

You must come to know who you really are before you can begin to properly establish yourself and your surroundings. Who you think you are may be a culmination of many events that have transpired in your life. Who you are may consist of what people have told you; in other words, who *people* think you are. Who you think you are may stem from how people have treated you. Who you believe you are may be centered around the circumstances that you have encountered. Regardless of who you think you are at this very moment, you have decided to believe that is who you are. Always remember – who you believe and say you are is who you will be. Perception is everything. How you view your life is up to you. Ultimately, how your life unfolds is your decision. As you flow through the messages between these pages, you will begin to understand the power that is invested in you. Power is the innate ability to govern your life. <u>Invest</u> simply means to devote.

Who Are You?

Therefore, you will begin to understand how investing in yourself helps you to embrace your power. Who has the power? YOU DO!

The scenario you are about to read pertains to a teenager who did not grasp the understanding of power and investment. The scenario arose because I was sharing with a colleague about a string of sessions that I was conducting on "Your Thoughts, Your Attitude, and Your Destiny." I will give the name Chasity to my colleague's image of this confused teenager for the sake of this book.

The abbreviated version of the scenario:

While discussing goals, the future, and desires of success, Chasity stated that she did not feel the need to participate in group discussion. Chasity boldly stated that she did not waste her time with dreaming because dreams did not come true. She stated that she could lose her freedom or her life tomorrow. My colleague described what he heard as a typical image of a confused teenager. If you were to encounter such a response what would go through your mind? How would you respond?

That was a thought provoking scenario from my colleague. In reality, Chasity represents many teens that I have encountered. The character represented in the scenario was seemingly lifeless. The following is what I explained to my colleague. Chasity's comment could be based on a several things. First, Chasity might not see beyond her drugs and gang infested neighborhood. In her desolate environment, she might not know whether she would live a full life or whether she would land herself in a spider web of swinging in and out of the judicial system.

Second, perhaps Chasity could not see beyond her current living situation; a living situation with no direction or love being imparted in her daily. Perhaps it's ALL she knows. Chasity could be a product of learned behaviors from the environment she was raised. Perhaps she saw some of her family member or neighbors either selling drugs, suffering from drug addictions, involved in gang activities, or living part time in the locked-up life (the judicial system). Maybe Chasity really did not know anything about the future or the possibility of a lavished lifestyle. Simply put, she could have been trying to survive in a world of defeat.

Third, Chasity could have been afraid to succeed or did not know how to succeed. Although she spoke death over her life, she wanted to live – just like you and me. She was crying out for help. You know how it is today; it is hard to do what is good and right because your peers and counterfeit friends might just make you feel like an outcast. It becomes more serious when your relatives do not want to see you succeed. Some of you have heard the infamous clichés: "You're not going to amount to anything, just like your Daddy" "I don't know why you're doing that, it's not going to work." "You are just wasting your time." "You can't do anything right." So what does this lead to? It leads to a destroyed self-esteem for many who hear such demeaning words. Not only that, but many people were never taught how to properly succeed.

Chasity's silent cry emerged through her negative and depressed comments. I heard Chasity saying, HELLO, IS ANYBODY OUT THERE, will you help me, because I have limited resources. My family can't seem to help me and I don't know what to do. There are a couple of supportive people in my life and they are doing the best they can, but I need more. I am borderline with being suspended or expelled from school. What I heard Chasity whisper was "Please, I need help. Can't you hear my cry?"

My thoughts actually serve as a precursor to how I would begin to address the concerning replies that were made by Chasity, which leads to answering another question, "What do you do?" When dealing with an individual that seemingly has lost the zest to live and succeed or a person who is bound by the fear of the unknown (the future), there is no "quick fix" remedy that man can offer. There are procedures and information that can be shared that will assist with getting the individual back on track. With knowing this, I have decided to interact with and speak to teenagers and young adults as often as possible. For these individuals, I have decided to place in print helpful information that can be referred to again and again when necessary.

Chasity was saying what many teens say at some point in their lives. Although not all teenagers' situations are as dramatic as the one about Chasity, they still may encounter a desolate place at some point in their life. Many youths are in that lost place right now. That "alone place" is where no one seems to understand and no one seems to care. But I am here to tell you that there are people that understand and there are definitely people that care. I understand and care about not just your well being today and tomorrow, but more importantly, I care about your future and eternal life.

So right now, you have the power to **STOP** believing the hype. Right now you might not be able to accomplish that alone. Because I understand and care, it is my intention to help you to understand who you really are. So keep reading.

Be mindful of what you choose to believe, for that which you believe in becomes you.
- ckendrick

Think for a minute. Who are you? Go ahead, be honest with yourself; it is just you and God listening. And I will let you in on a little secret, God already knows. So, again I ask, "Who are you?" Are you a dummy? Are you clumsy and always in the way? Are you going to amount to nothing just like your daddy? Hello young person, are you going to try to escape through the use of meth and aerosol cans? Are you destined to be cut out of the inheritance? Are you going to be a dropout too? Are you going to engage in gang and/or devil worshipping activities just like your older siblings or friends? Are you working on having two children before you are forced to drop out of high school? These are all legitimate questions that some teens may have an answer of yes to, because they are suffering just like Chasity. You may not really know who you are at times, because you have been receiving mixed messages throughout your life about who you are.

These mixed messages sometimes came from adults and authority figures that you looked up to and trusted.

Who you think you are might be what people have told you. So what have people been telling you? You have to reflect and ask yourself that question. You know what people told you. Some told you bad, ugly things. Some told you that you couldn't do it. Some told you that you wouldn't make it. Then some told you good things. Some told you to reach for the stars. Some told you that you were smart. Some told you that you would make it. The point is you received mixed messages. When mixed messages are received it causes some confusion.

Some people actually receive more negative commentaries spoken to them than positive comments. When this happens, we should start investing in ourselves by saying positive things about who we are. Simply feed yourself positive thoughts. You should always tell yourself positive things. This is your shield against negativity. For example, haven't you had someone tell you that you could not achieve something and you immediately replied by saying I can do it (and you had attitude when you responded). We tell ourselves positive things because our Creator is all positive. Because your Father is positive, you have inherited those dynamic and positive genes. Think about when people look at a baby and say, "She looks just like her mother." Well, I am here to tell you that we look just like our Father. Unfortunately, we have been tainted somewhat by people, life, and circumstances. But there is hope for our lives.

Again, who you think you are might be how people have treated you. Perhaps you have been treated like the misfit, the outcast, the mess-up. Some people have been haphazardly handled. Some people that crossed your path probably did not care how they addressed and labeled you. Seemingly, based on their actions, these people could care less about how they treated you and sent out sharp, painful visions to your spirit and mind. But **know** you are **great**! All people should be treated with dignity and respect, regardless of age. All people should be handled as if they were glass or precious cargo.

The lives of youths are like glass
Please Handle With Care

When we are shipping breakable items through the mail to loved ones, we make sure we place on the box "Fragile – Handle with Care". In actuality my Loves, you are fragile and breakable. My Loves, know that you are glass – the glass I am talking about is that of a diamond. You are a precious jewel to all whom you come in contact. It is up to them to recognize your worth. Remember that! I wish more of you knew your worth, because then you would not have to wear your bling-bling around your neck or in your ears to measure your worth. Your bling-bling is all over you and all in you. Wait…I am getting ahead of the book. I will tell you more about who you really are in a latter chapter.

Who you think you are might center on the circumstances that you were undeservingly placed in at times. Take the time to reflect on some of the fond times and circumstances you had that you were just blessed to be a part of - makes you feel good and even smile a bit, huh? Just as you reflect on those fond memories there are other times that you wish could be deleted forever from your memory. Although some of these circumstances occurred a long time ago, they can still cause your mood to change.

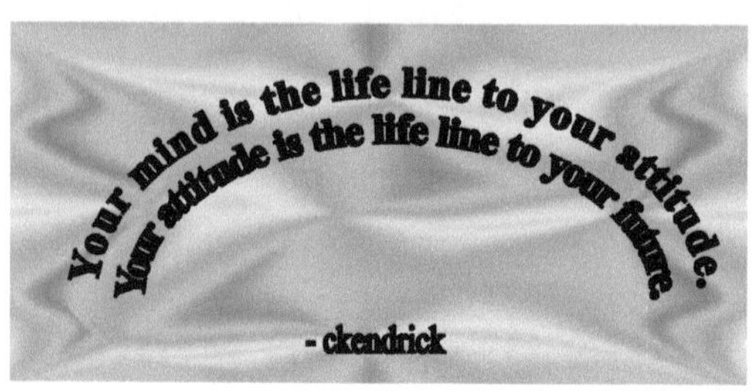

There are some young people who have to grow up in environments where they are seemingly the caretaker of their younger siblings. There are some circumstances that some young people are placed you in that hinder them from getting a good night's rest and receiving a complete breakfast to start each morning. Some teens' circumstances expose them to adult situations that they should not have to face. No, they did not ask for such circumstances, they were simply born into these environments. Before you and I were born, we had a purpose and a plan placed over our lives. If you are in a tough environment, it is not your permanent parking place; it is temporary, because tomorrow is a brand new day.

Who you are is your total make up; coupled with how you decide to handle and adjust to the life you have been blessed with. It is important to have a good attitude. Your mind is the life line to your attitude. Your attitude is the life line to your future. Your attitude will help you to rise up out of your negative circumstances. That's why it is important that you constantly strive to have a positive attitude. Yes, many of you have been birthed into some tough situations. Yes, many of you have received some really bad breaks. You have the power in you to make changes that will positively impact your future. Know that you are valuable, loved, and that there are brighter days ahead. Yes, your best days are ahead of you. Believe it. You have to start mentally and verbally acknowledging them.

You can not change the past. Although you can not change the past, one of your responsibilities is to learn from your past. The bad and ugly experiences, vow to not repeat those things in your life when you are able to start making adult decisions. Make those bad and ugly events a foot stool or rung in your ladder for you to climb as you reach your destiny. Take hold of and cherish the good experiences.

Who you think you are might be what people have told you. Who you think you are might be how people have treated you. Who you think you are might be what you have observed since birth. Who you think you are might center around the circumstances that you were undeservingly placed in at times. Who you are, is your past (your total make up), coupled with how you decided to handle and adjust to your current life's circumstances. You are more than the bad and ugly circumstances. As you read further in the other chapters you will really gain a better understanding about who you <u>really</u> are. Stop believing the negative commentary that has been spoken to you. You are so much greater than who you think you are most of the time. You are awesome!

Planting
and
Uprooting

Who Is Planting In Your Garden Of Life 2

When we begin to plant the smallest of flowers, we have to dig up the soil and then place the flower in the hole. Next, we water the area. This is as simple as it comes to gardening, but know that there are many more steps that can be incorporated. There are people you encounter on a regular basis that plant in your garden of life. Sometimes they simply plant in your garden without even asking permission.

Chasity, whom we read about in the previous chapter, simply represents many teenagers whose garden of life has been planted in by so many different types of people. These people bring different mind-sets, beliefs, values, and morals. Often times they do not quite understand how they are truly destroying the flower beds of young people. As they haphazardly cross young teens' thresholds, they fail to take care of these prized possessions.

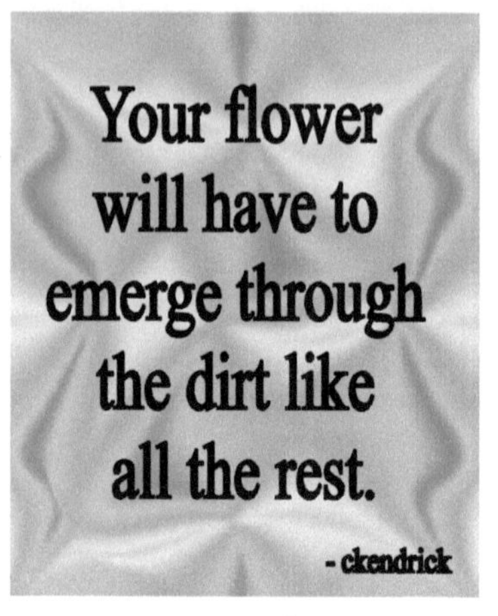

There were people that planted in your life during your earlier years and they may have left you with some not so good seeds. Their words and actions may have lowered your self-esteem and made you angry. Some teenagers and young adults are working through physical, mental, and emotional abuse, rejection, parental divorce, neglect, etc. You did not ask for these life challenges. You were not the cause of these reckless and insensitive acts. Nevertheless, you will have to grow through the dirt that was placed on you. Your flower will have to grow through the dirt like every other flower.

Let me shed some light on your garden. The sun shines on the bad seeds, just as it does on the good seeds. Rain falls on the poisonous plants, just as rain replenishes the non-poisonous ones. In spite of those selfish and ignorant planters in your life, you will survive and grow through your challenges and misfortunes. The sun shines and the rain falls on the good, the bad, and the ugly.

There are brighter, refreshing days ahead of you. There are planters who handle the flower beds with tender, love, and care. You have encountered some of those planters as well. They are called your positive planters. Often times we overlook these gardeners or can't see them for all the confusion and strife in our lives.

Become a more active seeker of these positive planters. Be on the look out for them. They are all around you. It was these positive planters that helped to create in you a positive path. Be thankful for the positive planters. It was their planting that helped get you to this point. You have had some good times in your life. For those people who can not recall any pleasant times from their past, they have simply buried their positive path under mounds of negative nightmares.

Your life is your prized possession. Your life is in your hands. You know it's fragile, so handle it with care. You are held accountable for your life, not your parents, guardians, teachers, etc. The positive caretakers and role models in your life are there to assist you through life. They will have to answer for their lives and how they assisted and treated you as they encountered you. Every adult and every young adult will have to answer for his or her own life. So why do we give so many people control over what we will ultimately be responsible for?

Although, others planted in your garden of life, know that the garden is still yours. It is your responsibility to take control over your life. I'll help you. First, take the gardening tools from the ignorant, sick, evil, and selfish adults who are hurting you and trying to destroy your life. You are not going to allow anyone to speak a negative word to you. They may say them, but you WILL NOT take them in. Every time a negative sentence comes, you tell yourself something positive.

Do it right then. You do not have to verbalize it right then, you can just say it in your mind. Let's try it.

Life Hater: You can't ever do anything right.

Awesome You: **I have skills. I am great at writing, singing, etc.**

Life Hater: I know you will not pass my class.

Awesome You: **I am smart. I will complete my work and pass.**

Life Hater: You will be locked up or dead within 5 years.

Awesome You: **My Lord created me in His image, and He will protect me. I am on a bright path. This hater has no control over my life.**

Every time someone speaks negatively to you, tell yourself positive things immediately. And if you just happen to reflect over their negative words later, please dismiss their words and treatment towards you and start reciting positive things about yourself. If you seem to have a mental block just recite the following:

I am beautiful.

I am loved.

I have a great future waiting on me.

I will be prosperous.

I am blessed.

I am smart.

I will overcome.

I am a survivor.

I am beautiful.

If these are not working and you need more, thumb through the chapter "Who You Really Are".

This is called uprooting and re-planting. By up-rooting you set the precedence of cleaning your life and planting goodies in it. You are the key gardener and you hold the gardening tools to your life. You will determine how things will be planted in your life. You will determine how the upkeep of your garden will look. I can already see the beauty forming in your garden.

Take those life destroyers and negative influencers and kick them out of your garden. Now, put up a NO-TRESPASSING sign. What you are doing here is establishing your boundaries. You are not allowing anyone to come back into your life if their purpose is to hurt and destroy you. You are saying, I will not allow you to hurt me anymore." Note - those negative planters are not necessarily the people you call enemies or haters. For clarity, some children's parents speak negative words to them and do hurtful things. So if your mother says to you, "You are just going to end up in jail like your father." She is speaking a negative word into your spirit and soul. Then you have to say something positive to yourself, "I have a bright future and I will be successful and law abiding." Your church member may say, "Baby, make sure you keep your job at McDonald's, because times are tough and there is nothing else out there for you." You must say, "I am talented. I have skills. I will be successful and better doors will open up for me."

I am reminded of an old movie. There was this male child whose mother did not raise him. He was raised during many of his teen years by this foster parent. She was extremely mean to him. She was verbally and emotionally abusive. While residing with this foster parent, the child was molested by a relative of the foster parent who resided there as well. He runaway and became homeless at some point in his life. Finally, he was old enough to work, so he enlisted in the military. He struggled with anger problems among other things, which kept him in trouble. The words of advice that were finally provided to him, as he began to get his life on track, were that he needed to address his past and close some doors to the past.

This young man visited three people, his foster mother, the molester, and his biological mother. His closure with the foster mother and her daughter was simply to inform them that they were kicked out of his garden. He basically told them you will never ever again plant in my garden. He showed them that despite every mean and hateful thing they did to him, when he was young and helpless, he still survived. He was a good person, and has a bright future. The last look he gave each of them basically told them that he had a NO TRESPASSING sign up just for them.

This gentleman visited his biological mother for another reason. Seemingly, he needed some closure with a person that he felt should have protected him, cared for him, and planted positive seeds in his garden of life. He had to address rejection face-to-face. He learned that his biological mother had lifetime bouts with drugs and the judicial system. His questions to his mother centered on why did she give him away? Why did you not come back for me? Then he felt the need to tell her about his success and happiness. His mother had no answers or responses of any true substance for him.

This young man was taking control of his garden. This young man understood the importance of: 1) bringing closure to his past, 2) taking back his life and taking control of it, 3) not allowing his past to dictate his future, and 4) how changing his mind-set and attitude will change his life. Do not allow your past to define who you are. You are a person with a past. Your past should not dictate who you are today. Your past will not dictate who you will be tomorrow.

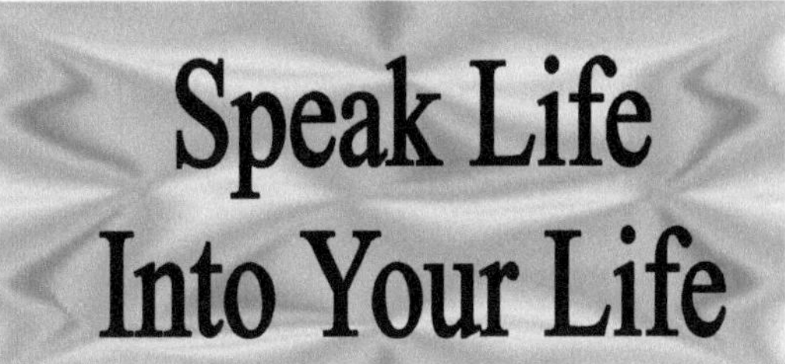

There are so many people in this world that have been hurt and rejected mostly by loved ones, not their enemies. So, identify the negative words from your past and replace them with positive life-giving words. Recognize your progress to a better you. Your future is bright. From this point on, when those people attempt to make you feel like a "nobody", you are to say "I am somebody, for my life is important and necessary."

You have the power to bring closure to all the negative circumstances that happened in your life. From this day forward, you have the power to rebuild and rectify your life. You were created to have a happy, healthy, and prosperous life, but you have to do some maintenance work at times on your life. Start today on speaking life into your life. We have lived long enough with speaking death and destructive things into existence in our lives.

Did you know that you can bring something into existence? All inventors first had a thought about something that was not yet reality. Then they starting working on bringing that thought to reality. Today we have energy operated cars, laptops, iPods, mp3 players, androids, e-tablets, and all types of shoes and clothing. Your thoughts plus action equals manifestation.

In the past, people were planting destruction in others lives every time they spoke something negative about them or mistreated them. They were destroying their spirits and souls. Guess what? Some people started living out those things that were repeatedly spoken to them. So it works like this – take Billy's life for example:

(The Negative Result)

In Phase 1

- Someone tells Billy that he is not going to make it.
- Someone else tells him that he is just a waste.
- He hears later that he is like the other males in his family – jail bound.

In Phase 2

- Billy began to tell himself that it doesn't matter anyhow.
- Billy says no one cares and he even meditates on it.

- He thinks no one expects him to do better so he is going to stop trying.

In Phase 3

- Billy actually starts causing small problems.
- Billy finds himself getting into trouble and according to his frame of thinking "they made him do it, if they would have just left him alone."
- Now he has authority figures giving him ultimatums like the next time you will be suspended, locked up, etc.
- Doors started closing for Billy and people began to stop associating with him (the people that were moving in the positive direction).

In Phase 4

- Billy has actually caught up with those initial words that were spoken over his life.

A Thought Is The Beginning To Reality
- ckendrick

- Billy has allowed them to become reality and he was an active participant.
- Billy spoke negative words over his life and doors closed. His opportunities and chances in life lessened.

Billy not only represents so many middle school and high school teenagers, but also Billy represents thousands of young adults who are serving many years of their lives in jail or prison right now. Can you see how you are ultimately responsible for your life and that you will be held accountable for it? Know that a thought is the beginning of reality. Your reality is what you think on most often, and what you think of yourself. You bring your reality into existence. So if you do not want a reality of hardship, pain, frustration and anger, do not plant negative thoughts, and do not allow others to plant negative thoughts in your mind.

You have the power to reap positive results. Imagine yourself being an Irrigation Engineer of your life. You may wonder what is an irrigation engineer? Let's break it down…You have a garden which represents your life. To keep your garden healthy and fruitful (productive) it has to have water along with a way for the water to pass throughout your garden. Thus, you will have to build an irrigation system to flush the dead old things out and bring in fresh nutritional things. The same thing applies to our lives. We must install a system that flushes out the old negative thoughts, as well as, brings in positives thoughts to nourish your garden of life. This is what irrigation engineers do, and you are the irrigation engineer of your garden.

Let's get back to uprooting, rebuilding, and changing. You can change your world one thought at a time. It is up to you to really determine what kind of world you want to have and live in for the rest of your life. For some of you right now your world looks pretty good. That's good, but do not settle for just good. Let's kick it up a notch and take it to great. Say, "My life will be great." Now say, "My life is great." You have started the process of forming your irrigation system.

Know that you are powerful. You were blessed and created with so much power. You have the power to call something that is non-existent into existence. You have the mental ability to direct your present and future. It is all in the way you think. It is all in the way you decide to view yourself. By planting one positive thought at a time, when good things happen to you, and when not so good things happen to you, you will create a new you each day.

With one positive thought planted you have already begun to change your world. Some people are under the impression that others make them who they are. They are who they are based on how they processed the way others handled them. They are who they are because they made many, many decisions along their path in life.

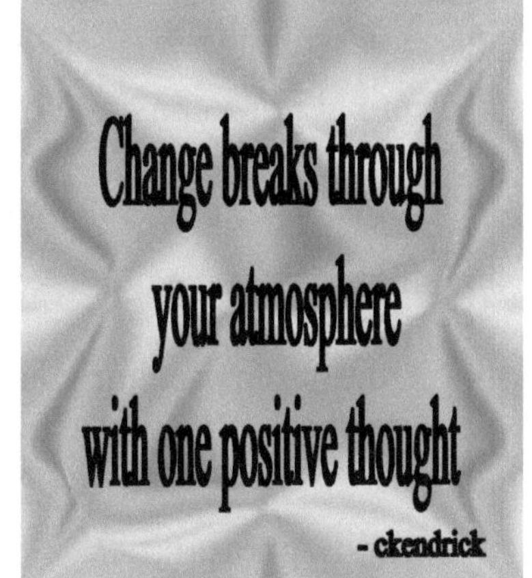

Since Billy demonstrated to you how powerful thoughts are in the negative, see how the power of thoughts can bring things into reality in your favor in this second example.

(The Positive Result)

In Phase 1

- Someone tells you that you are not going to make it.
- Someone tells you that you are just a waste.
- Someone tells you that you will be just like the others in your family – a failure.

In Phase 2

- You tell yourself you are already making it. You are seeing positive strides in your life each day.
- You tell yourself and others I am likeable, talented, and I can not wait to see the fruits of my labor, because I am a hard worker.
- You tell yourself and everyone that will listen, "I know who I am and the failures of others' lives will not cause me to get off my path."
- You go on to say, "I am on a good, healthy, law abiding path that is going to take me to some really good places in my life."

In Phase 3

- You actually start working harder in life, in school, on the job, and at home, in spite of your environmental challenges.
- You find your self being asked to assist and do helpful things that your were not asked to do before.
- Others start seeing your talents and your inner beauty.
- Doors start opening for you and you begin to receive really good opportunities.

In Phase 4

- Your reputation has actually caught up with **your** initial words that you spoke over your life.
- Your spoke words of life and you gave yourself life.
- Doors opened for you and you seized the moment.

Life grants people the opportunity to choose which path will be taken. There is more than one path in life. With every decision we make, we move further along our path.

Now let me share with you a scenario. There are these sisters who were born to the same mother and father and have been raised in the same home all their lives. The older sister was a successful student throughout high school. She was academically sound and she was not a disciplinary problem. Her younger sister, of three years, seemingly is the complete opposite. Yet these siblings were raised under the same circumstances.

The younger sister (let's call her Heather for the sake of this book) was a school tyrant. If it violated a rule, she did it. If it was said it could not be done, she tested it. Unfortunately, she made many poor decisions. Prior to finally entering high school, Heather had a history already with the juvenile justice system.

Why were these sisters seemingly so different? Know that there are multiple answers to this question. But I can attest to the fact that Heather's sister made a conscious decision and effort to make life better for herself. Heather's sister evidently understood some of the same things that the young gentleman did from the movie I previously mentioned. Heather's sister obviously knew that her attitude would either close or open doors for her. Heather's sister evidently did not allow and is not allowing her environment, past, challenges, and negative planters dictate how her

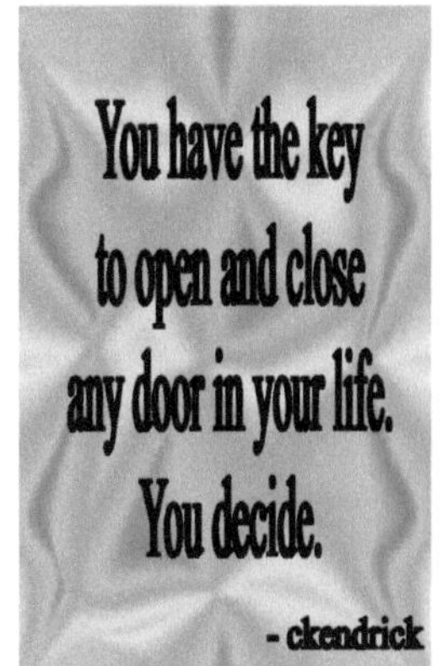

life will unfold. She made conscious decisions to have a successful and fulfilling life.

Also, I can attest to the fact that Heather is not making conscious choices and efforts to make her life better. Heather is trudging further and further off her proper path because of the decisions she makes, but she may have become lost in her past. Perhaps Heather is so different from her sister, because she has not 1) brought closure to her past and present hurts and pains, 2) taken control of her life - she is truly out of control, 3) taken back her life from the planters that planted negative seeds in her life – the negative beliefs about her are embedded in her mind still, and 4) learned that if she changed her mind-set and attitude that this will help to change her life.

Because some people are raised in environments infested with barriers, does not mean that those individuals do not stand a chance of surviving and being successful. Your environment DOES NOT define you who are nor who you will become. You can survive the toughest of tough situations. Many successful people have experienced similar environments. They survived and are living fulfilling and happy lives. Determination saved them. They were determined to make a brighter future for themselves. You are empowered. You were given the power to choose. You have dominion over your attitude. You are the gardener in your garden.

To Be or Not To Be... 3

Turning Discord into Reward

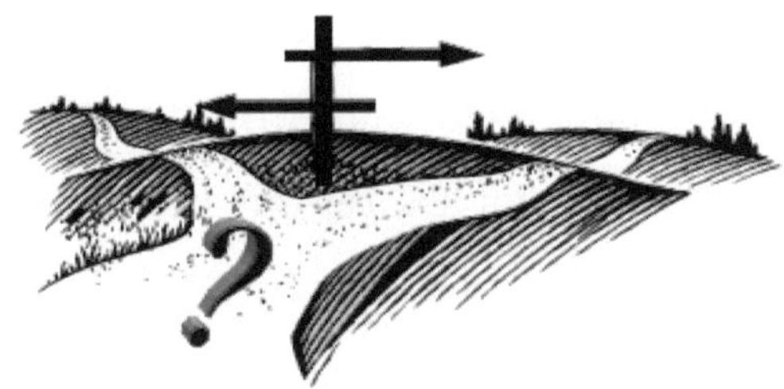

Everyone makes choices everyday and all day. You have the choice to be or not to be anything and everything you want to be. Your choices will determine your destination at the end of your day and at the end of your journey. Each day, your journey mentally begins with a thought. Each day, your journey physically begins with a step. You have the power to step off into your future each day you are granted life. Your future is determined by the attitude you decide to embrace every moment, every day. You have the choice as to how you will display your attitude each day. It is up to you to be or not to be defeated.

To Be or Not To Be...Lifeless

Turning Discord into Reward

> **Life owes you nothing, because you are indebted to it.**
> - ckendrick

You do not want to be defeated. No one wants to be defeated and lifeless. It is in your nature to want to prevail, reign, succeed, and survive. Let's get to the point. Life is not fair. Life may have dealt you a bad hand. Life sometimes seems as if it is not worth living. You did not ask for this life, but you are indebted to it. Life owes you nothing, but you owe your life everything. You will be paying life for the rest of your life. Life can be challenging. As Langston Hughes described it "Life ain't No Crystal Stair."

Life just might appear to have been all those things at some point in your journey. Yes, you have encountered negative nightmares, but you have also encountered positive past events. Unfortunately, our mind gravitates to the negatives quicker than it gravitates to the positives. What actually happens is that the mind is quicker to upload events that are coupled with strong emotions.

When a life event is coupled with strong emotions, some people will always be able to recall the event, as if it happened yesterday. For instance, some people can quickly recall when they were severely whipped for something they did not do, or when they were physically abused. They could also recall the surrounding smell, whether or not it was sunny or cloudy, because strong emotions were involved. The same uploads occur with positive events if they are coupled with strong emotions. Some individuals can remember hitting the winning shot of a basketball game that took place 20 years earlier. They can give play by play action for the last 3 minutes of the game. Well for them, that positive accomplishment was attached to some really strong, happy feelings.

You carry the power in you to be whatever you want to be

Unfortunately, it appears as though negative events come with strong emotional attachments a lot more often. But now that you have been schooled on how the mind works in this area, you should be able to download more positive events to your repertoire and keep more negative events from being committed to lifetime memory. When positive events happen in your life, make yourself become extremely excited about them. Overflow with excitement and joy. When negative events arise, address them in a positive manner, keep control, and respond if needed. Simply address the situation and move on. If these techniques are utilized, you will be on your way to planting positive memories for your future and keeping negative memories from taking over your life.

You carry the power in you to be whatever you want to be. What you allow into your life will determine what you will become. What you speak into your life will also determine what you will become. If you want to forever be chased by discord or friction in your life then hang around negative planters. If you want to be forever surrounded by reward, then place positive planters in your life.

It is up to you to determine your outcomes. I have never encountered anyone who wanted to have friction and stress in his life.

Although no one wants a life filled with friction and stress, many people make decisions that reap these things. This happens because these individuals allow negatives to be spoken into their lives. They bring stress into their lives because of what they place their attention on. Whatever has your attention will be what affects your life, so focus your attention on that which edifies and not that which destroys. Where you place your attention will determine whether or not you reap discord or reward.

Let go of your past to receive your future

You do not want to create discord in your life. No one wants a sad and frustrating life. It is your nature to want to have a successful and flourishing life. Sometimes you have to lose in order to gain. When you open your hands to let go of the past, that same hand is open to receive your future. To avoid discord in your life, you should merely open up to letting go of the past. When you become open to letting go, the future will rush into your life. Open your hand. Let go. Open up the doorways to your future.

Your life is the make up of all that is placed in it. It could be left empty, packed with negative fillers, or packed with positive fillers. Imagine a box that is being packed to be shipped to you. You can decide what you would like to receive in your box. You have the right to ask that nothing be placed in your box if you want the sender to send you an empty box. You may be satisfied with just having a box. Some people may decide that their box to be filled with negative fillers. The items that are placed in this box are all those things that can quickly or slowly cause even more chaos to come into your life and destroy it. Or your gift box could be filled with things that bring life and joy. You can decide to have your box filled with a bundle of life enhancing items; things that can quickly or slowly bring happiness and success to you. What will you decide to have in your box? What would you like shipped to you?

Your box is your box-of-life. You will get what you decide you want. If you decide you want to have an empty life, then that is what will come to you. If your decision is to have a life that is filled with continued chaos and discord, then be prepared to be miserable. Continued chaos and misery can actually drain the life out of life. You have the authority to choose to have your box-of-life filled to capacity with enhancing life-agents that opens doors to reward, joy, and success.

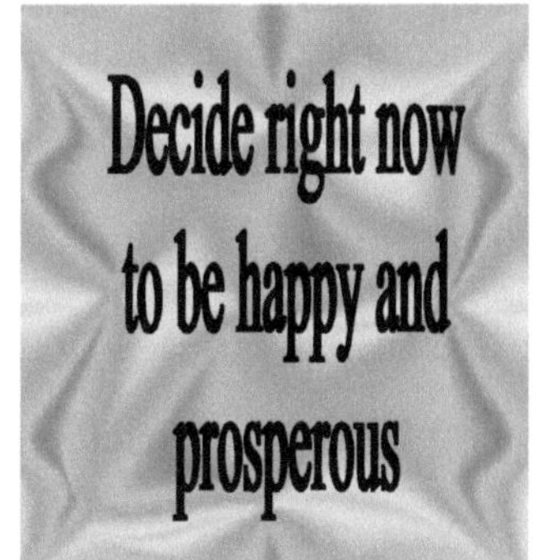

For individuals that do not possess boxes-of-life that are packed with positive fillers here are some helpful pointers. Remember, space can be replaced and the negatives can be turned into positives. If your box is empty, decide right now to be somebody. Decide this moment to be happy and prosperous. When you decide to have a fulfilled life, then you can begin to place positive thoughts, images, dreams, circumstances, etc. into your space. Space is placed before you on a silver platter in order for you to do whatever you want to with it. It is your space, your box-of-life. Enjoy it. Have fun with it. Live righteously with it. Fulfill it. *Full-fill* it with love and happiness.

The hardest step to filling space is beginning. It is hard sometimes to do things that seemingly may require a little work and effort. All that needs to be done is to start speaking positive thoughts and words into your life. For those of you that are empty box individuals, no one else is needed to get started. You simply tell yourself that you are successful, happy, financially stable, mentally stable, healthy, etc. Now that you have gotten past the hardest step of beginning, you will continue to press forward. As you feed yourself positive thoughts repeatedly, you will begin to feel better about yourself, and then you will become more active in not allowing others to speak negative words about you, to you.

Disallowing people to speak negative words over you is a part of the life filling process that does involve others. In this phase you will have to be more conscious about what you allow people to say to you. Now you are placing life into your space. Now you are waking up your empty and lifeless body. You are taking back control of your life. You have the power to control what you allow to enter and affect you. When you control what you allow to enter and affect you, then you have control. This is the first step to taking your life back. Again,

**Control what you allow to enter and affect you,
then you have control.
This is the first step to taking your life back.**

- ckendrick

this is your space. This is your box-of-life. Take it back. Do some remodeling. It belongs to you; fill it full with thoughts, words, and actions that will bring you reward and happiness forevermore.

To address individuals that have boxes that are sitting before them, packed with negative fillers, change is good. Negatives can be turned into positives. If your box is overflowing with negativity, you are reaping undue stress and discord in your life. You have to decide right now to let go of the negative and latch on to your fruitful future. You have to want change and you have to be determined to change.

You want to acquire rewards in your life. You are ready to be compensated in life. You want your life back; you do not want to be lifeless. It is your season and time to collect rewards in your life. Your life was filled with reward before you were born. Favor was placed on your life before you ever breathed earth's air. You brought with you, into this world, the opportunity to be happy and successful. What you are to do is open the gift that was already given to you. Open up your life. Open up to life. Allow your life to be a thoroughfare for reward to freely flow in and out of it.

To be or not to be…lifeless that is the question. What is your answer? You possess the power to make the decision that you WILL be filled with life. You WILL overcome discord with reward. You WILL be happy. You WILL be successful. YOU WILL BE

REWARDED. You are valuable. You are necessary. Your life is necessary.

Your harvest time is right now. It is time for you to reap reward. Reward is waiting on you. It is up to you whether or not you receive it. It is a decision that you have to make. You decide how happy and successful you want to be. You decide to what degree you will allow blessings to enter your life. All you have to do is decide how you are going to complete the cliché "To be or not to be…" All you have to do is decide which box-of-life you will receive.

It's Your Decision
How You Handle Your Life

You can decide to follow it or lead it.

You can decide to hate it or love it.

You can decide to close it or open it.

You can decide to reject it or accept it.

You can decide to lose it or choose it.

You can decide to leave it or receive it.

You can decide to ignore it or recognize it.

You can simply decide to love it and live it.

– **C. Kendrick**

To Have or Not To Have... 4

Turning Strife into Life

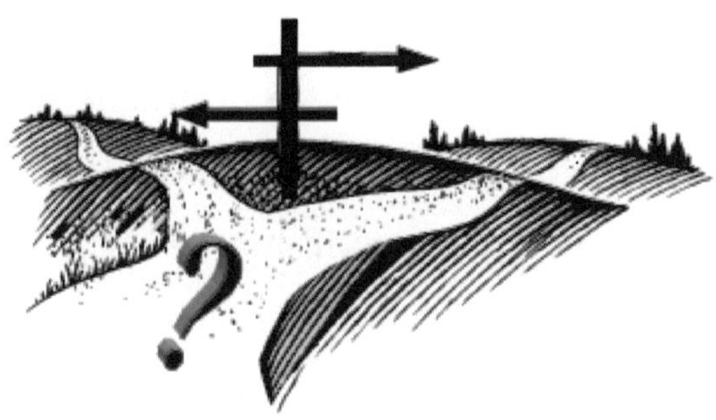

Choices have to be made everyday. You make the choice to have or not to have anything and everything you want in life. Your choices will determine your destination at the end of your day. Will you end up with what you needed and desired? Each day your life's journey begins with a thought. You can rise to the thoughts of wanting to have sweet abundant life, or to cause bitter strife. Your thoughts and thought process can move you into embracing life and dismissing any strife that may come your way. Each day you are granted life, you determine whether or not you will have or will not have the sweetness that life offers. Your destiny of

To Have or Not To Have...

Turning Strife into Life

having is determined by the attitude you decide to embrace every moment, every day. Your attitude, the way you address circumstances, will determine what you will acquire. It is up to you to have or not have peace, joy, love, and success.

Friction in life is called strife. Strife is synonymous to conflict, trouble, and resistance. How you choose to handle and address your strife in life is going to determine how much you are going to have, or how much you will not have. How you address strife will determine how far you excel in life. Some people feel that it is their duty to reap havoc and cause stress in the lives of others. These people make conscious efforts to ensure that another person is uncomfortable, afraid, and beaten. Actually many people start their morning with deciding that they are going to make someone else's day miserable. That is their only SORRY mission.

For example, Kim decides that she does not like Marsha. She just wants to make Marsha's day horrific. That is her mission. She thought about her all day. She talked about her all night to anyone who would listen, like her flunky Kelly. Kelly has joined the club of misery. They waste time plotting and planning how they will create strife in Marsha's life. As they pass Marsha in the hallway they make cunning, threatening remarks. Kim can not focus on class work, because she has allowed all of her energies to be directed at Marsha. Finally, in the classroom, Kim gets a moment to reap havoc. She and Kelly taunt Marsha throughout the class period. Marsha does not respond to the ignorance, but she does inform the teacher. As class ends, Kim and Kelly leave somewhat joyous, because they believe they have accomplished their mission. They decide to carry out the same sad and immature process tomorrow. Kim and Kelly have no life. I hope I have not described you, but I believe you know someone just like Kim and Kelly. Some people thrive on creating strife in the lives of others.

Let me share what really happens in situations like the aforementioned scenario. Kim is actually the one living in misery. She is sad, broken, and miserable. She simply wants someone to experience pain, because she is actually hurting. Most often, this type of situation manifests because females are jealous and envious. A female may become jealous of another person because that person may possess something that she feels she should have. These females tend to become jealous because others seemingly have outer beauty, personality, inner beauty, intelligence, popularity, success, or simply a life without friction. These females have surrendered their power. They are actually the powerless losers because they are being controlled.

Kim and Kelly were actually being controlled by Marsha because they spent all of their time thinking about and talking about her. That gives Marsha the power. Marsha actually controlled their day. Marsha had them both thinking about and stressing over her all

How you address stress in life
will help determine how far you excel in life

day and all night, while she was enjoying her life. Kim and Kelly were bothered. They could not rest, because they were so focused on Marsha – Marsha, Marsha, Marsha. They could not take their minds off Marsha long enough to turn in quality work to the teacher. And more than likely, Kim and Kelly would eventually get into trouble with either school officials or the law, because they are so fixated on warping Marsha's day. It just depends on how far they allow their stupidity and ignorance to linger out of control.

Just like there are some people who feel that it is their duty to reap havoc in others' lives, there are other people who allow havoc to be reaped and to linger in their lives. All of us are confronted with conflict during our lifetime. It is how we handle the strife that is the determining factor to life's continuation path. The way conflict is addressed is going to determine the outcome. The attitude that is displayed is going to help move you into your desired destiny or it is going to hinder you from obtaining what you desire.

People have peace and joy in their life because they have learned and utilized the formula – positive attitude plus positive response equal positive outcomes (**PA + PR = PO**). Positive outcomes include those things you need, desire, and just love having. Positive outcomes are like Prego – it's in there. Positive out comes are all encompassing. With the positive attitude couple with positive responses you reap reward, peace, joy, power over the enemy, control over the enemy, success, growth, etc. It is vital that you understand the power of thinking and being positive and having a positive attitude. It is one of the main keys to your future.

To *"have not"* is not the in thing. To have not is stressful and causes people to worry. It is a dreadful feeling, when you do not have something that you need or want. To have not is partially due to mental poverty. An impoverished mind is what causes those that were gifted with intelligence to become dumb; those that were blessed into the midst of wealth to become poor; those that were graced with beauty to become ugly; and those that were equipped with strength to become weak. An impoverished mindset is a mind that has not been properly fed. An impoverished mindset lacks nutrients. You nourish your mind with the nutrients of positive thoughts and actions. Negative thoughts and negative actions distort and deform the mind. Many people are roaming this earth with distorted and impoverished minds. That's scary, but true. Don't you become one of those people. It's when you invest in positive thoughts and positive actions that you begin to properly grow.

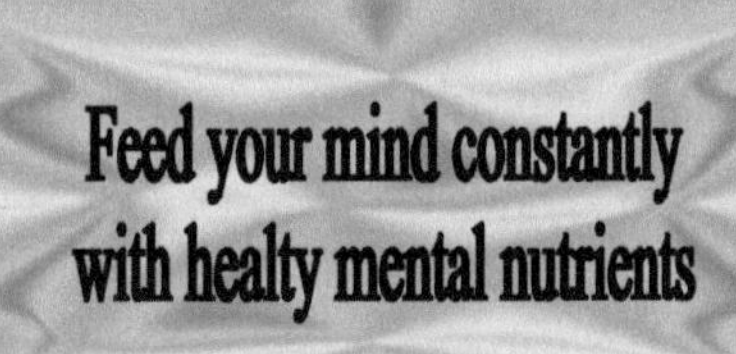

You must invest in positive thinking. You must feed your mind daily. You can not afford to miss a meal. Feed your mind positive breakfast when you wake up. Nourish your mind with positive lunch and snacks as you roam infested and impoverished settings. Feed your mind with a nutritious dinner for each day you will come in contact with negative planters, whose primary purpose is to put you in mental poverty and keep you there. Do not forget misery loves company. Protect yourself from infestation, poverty, and negative planters by planting good seeds in your life. For those of you who love to eat, yet worry about your weight, you can eat positive foods day and night and not have to worry about obesity, calories, cholesterol, trans fats, etc. And they digest well. Eat, eat, eat, positive foods. When your life becomes filled with positive thoughts and actions, you will start to reap your life's wishes. You will incur the good things in life and have them in abundance.

You must be the head gardener in your life. Do not relinquish your life to others, especially the negative planters, and then become upset with the outcome. Hold yourself responsible for you life. Others are holding you responsible for it. Please know that an impoverished mindset leads to death and destruction, for an impoverished mindset has been contaminated with negative seeds. Please believe that a healthy mindset is a positive mind that is constantly being feed positive thoughts. Please believe that positive outcomes are direct results of positive thoughts and actions. That which you believe today will surely affect that which you achieve tomorrow.

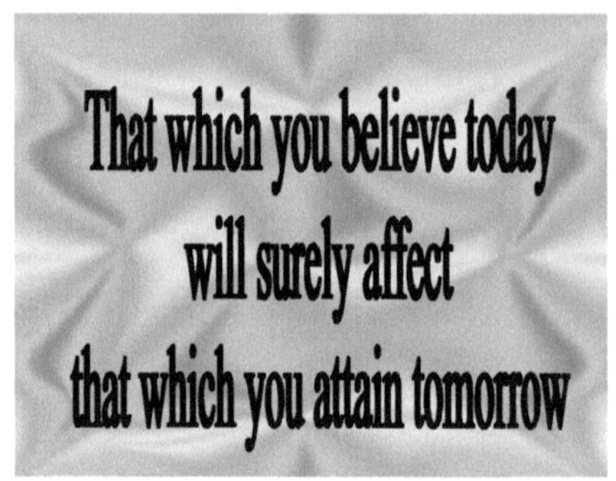

Almost everyone has had to deal with negative planters in their past. The vast majority of people have had to encounter unwarranted, negative circumstances at some point during their life. Too often we focus on the past instead of aiming for the possibilities ahead. Look forward, to that which is in front of you. Tomorrow is gone. Decide to have great abundance in your life, and when this decision is made, you will find that you will receive more than you could have ever thought or asked. If you simply do what is right. If you plant positive seeds in your life and into the lives of others, all of your needs will be met. So do not focus on your past, focus on the opportunities ahead of you.

It is up to you to determine your outcomes. No one enjoys a life filled with strife. No one wakes up everyday and wants to encounter sadness, stress, and struggle. No one, not even the individuals like Chasity, Kim, and Kelly wakes up asking for life's disappointments. Everyone wants to experience peace in their life. Everyone wants to have fun and happiness in their days. Many people simply become caught up in the drama of circumstances. Life just happened and they had no control over much of it. Life happened and it scared them. Scars heal. Life goes on. You decide where your life goes from here. You have the power to decide. You control your destiny.

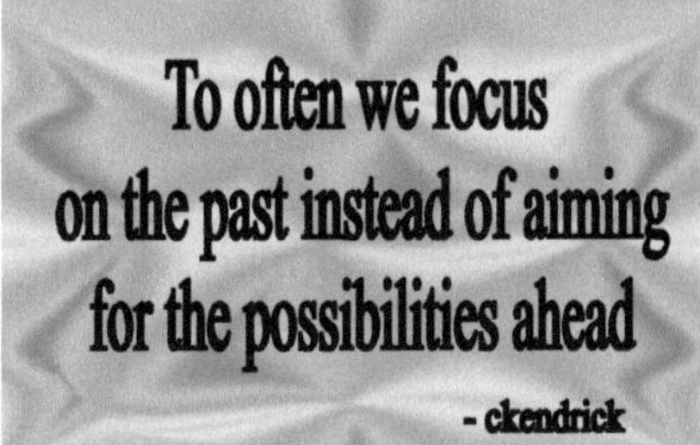

As mentioned in the previous chapter, open up your life. Open up to life. Allow your life to be a thoroughfare for reward to freely flow in and out of it. Take the limits off your life. Henry Ford once said, "Whether you think that you CAN, or that you CAN'T…you are right!" You bring into your world whatever you believe is possible, or whatever you believe you can be or have. If you think you can, then you will. You can acquire the riches that life wants to give you, if you think you can. You will acquire a life of rewards when you know you can. Do not become one of those people that does not have because you put limitations on yourself. No limits. Place no limits on what you will receive, because you have the power to stop limiting yourself. Remove the shackles.

You are ready to possess the good things in life. You are ready to have the desires of your heart. You are ready to experience the sweetness and beauty that comes with life on a consistent basis. You are ready to experience these things each day, not just every once in awhile. Since you are expecting the sweet taste of life, set your expectations high. Dream and dream big! Expect to possess tangible and intangible wealth above imagination. Tell yourself you deserve it. Now go out and start earning it. The more effort planted, the more you will reap. Work hard. Continuously plant positive seeds. To everything we obtain, effort is necessary. You are indeed privileged to possessing the good things in life.

You are equipped with the power to make the decision that you WILL have the goods and riches that were promised to you. You were promised these things before you were born into this world. You WILL overcome strife in life. You WILL be prosperous. You WILL be successful. YOU WILL HAVE YOUR HEART'S DESIRES. You will have all your needs met. Do your part. Take ownership of your life. Do what is right. Be positive. Speak positive words to yourself. Feed yourself. Feed others.

You are in a ripe season. Take advantage of it. The good life awaits you. It is up to you whether or not you receive it. It is a decision that you have to make. You decide what you want to acquire and how much you want to acquire. You determine to what degree you will allow blessings to enter your life. Your "haves" are in your hands.

What You Have In Life Depends On You

You can have life and have it more abundantly too;
An abundant life is dependant on you.

You can have life, with more success too;
A successful life is dependant on you.

You can have life, with more wealth too;
A wealthy life is dependant on you.

You can have life, with more joy too;
A joyous life is dependant on you.

You can have life, with more peace too;
A peaceful life is dependant on you.

You can have life, with more love too;
A loving life is dependant on you.

You Can Have It All
Make the Choice

– C. Kendrick

Why Follow When You Can Lead

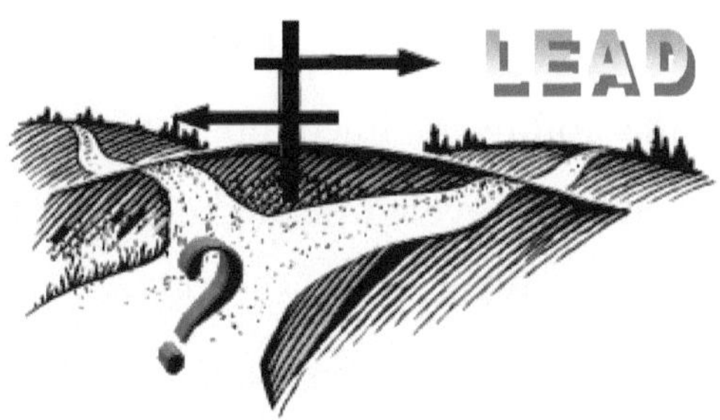

Why follow when you can lead? Perhaps people follow when they ought to be leading because that is what they have been taught most of their lives. Come here. Go there. No. Stop. Speak when spoken to. Do as I say do. A command is issued to them and like a rabbit they jump to it. Some people decide not to ever lead in anything throughout their lifetime, simply because they do not think they are competent. These particular individuals are merely bound by fear. Some of them are afraid to fail and some of them are afraid to succeed. Now believe that – yes, some people are actually afraid of success. Then there are people who decide not to lead, because they have a below water level self esteem. They do not believe they are capable. These individuals have settled for mediocrity. They do not believe in themselves and the power that is invested in them. There are many reasons why some people choose to be followers all their lives and shy away from being a leader.

I can recall a game I played as a child. The name of the game was *Follow the Leader*. I played this game for years. It was a simple game that required no real thinking. The leader was the person in front of the line and the followers lined up behind the leader. As we walked, ran, jumped and traveled throughout the play area, the leader made all the decisions. Whatever the leader did, the followers would all have to imitate the same actions and movements. If the leader determined that you did not imitate the movement properly, then you would be out of the game until the game started over.

Unfortunately, the leader would most of the time be the older participants. If you were liked, or liked on that day, you may get a chance to lead. I was one who yearned to lead as often as possible. Although I was much younger than most of the children in the neighborhood, I got the chance to lead on a regular basis. I wanted to lead. To me, that was the goal of the game – to lead.

There were children who actually did not mind being the followers. I believe they were complacent with just being a part of the game. I could not understand why someone would play such games and never desire to lead. It was so baffling that I often asked the followers, why follow, when you can lead? I would receive answers such as, I just don't want to, or I just want to stay here (in his/her designated spot as a follower). I truly believed that they wanted to lead, but were afraid to ask. I would often intervene and ask that they be allowed to lead. I would even offer that they lead in my place.

Their answers mesmerized me. They would still decline the offer to lead. I did not understand their thought process; it truly baffled me for years.

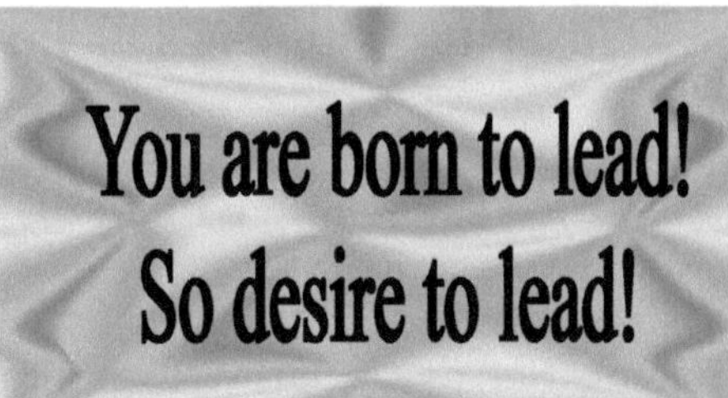

Today, I understand that a lot of answers could be provided as to why these individuals had no desire to lead. Some answers include, they did not want the responsibility of leading others, and did not desire anything other than their designated followers' positions. Perhaps their low self-esteem would not allow them to believe they were worthy of being first in line. Perhaps being told what to do and how to do everything in their lives up to that point did not lend itself to showing them they too could make decisions. After all, we were still children and as children we were often told what to do and what not to do. Perhaps they were not allowed to make decisions on their own, therefore, they never learned how the decision making process worked. At age 5, being allowed to select what you would wear for the day was a start to the decision making process. Now I better understand the many different possibilities that would hinder people's growth to the point that they would decide not to lead.

Still today, I believe deep down inside, the children that chose not to participate as a leader in the *Follow the Leader* game truly wanted to lead. They were born to lead and they wanted to lead. Unfortunately, at that point in their lives either their leadership capabilities were inhibited by negative planters or they had yet to be taught how to bring out their leadership skills.

Replace the follower's mentality with the leader's mentality

We were really young children then, being in that shy, fearful little world of "I can't do it" was okay for the moment, but as we grew to approach the pre-teen, teen, and young adult states, we had to put away that "little-girl" and "little-boy" shyness and lack of confidence. In life we are expected to develop through events and stages. We are expected to grow. We are expected to move through each stage of our life and through each event in our life gaining more wisdom, determination, and maturity. As we mature, we are held more accountable for our actions.

As we take on more responsibilities and as we are held more accountable, we should wash away that follower's mentality and replace it with a leader's mentality. A follower's mentality as a child is good and expected. A follower's mentality as a teen and young adult could be detrimental as you grow older. As your age increases, so should your level of maturity, knowledge, and responsibility.

Being a follower as a teen and young adult tends to reveal much about a person, and it is not just about fitting in with peers. Followers merely do what they are told to do. Followers are typically non-thinkers. They want others to think for them. They want others to dictate their life. In essence, followers surrender their lives to whomever they decide will lead them. You see – if it is making decisions that you are running from, then run Forest run, because you will not escape having to make decisions. Followers are typically lazy. Followers tend to possess low self-esteem. Followers just want to stay in that baby, child-like state that allows them to be free of accountability and decision making. When situations do not end on a positive note, followers are the first to ensure that the blame is placed on the leader. The mind-set of followers tells them that the situation will not end on a positive note. They look for things to go wrong. They expect it.

Being a leader as a teen and young adult reveals much about a person, and it has nothing to do with peers, but everything to do with the individual. Leaders are thinkers and dreamers that put their thoughts into action. Leaders are future seekers and visionaries. Leaders want to be in charge of others' lives. Leaders embrace responsibility. Leaders hold themselves accountable. Leaders are shakers and movers. Leaders are go-getters and they are definitely not lazy. Leaders tend to know who they are or that they are on the right path to searching and finding out who they are. Leaders are confident and possess a healthy sense of worth. Leaders know they are valuable jewels. Leaders long for growth. They are not stagnant people.

Unlike followers, leaders know that mistakes will be made and are ready to take the blame for attempting to reach new heights. The mind-set of leaders tells them that mistakes bring them one step closer

to success. They try another route when the outcomes do not emerge as planned, but they expect situations to come to fruition as planned. They expect it. They make decisions, execute the plan, and they expect positive end results.

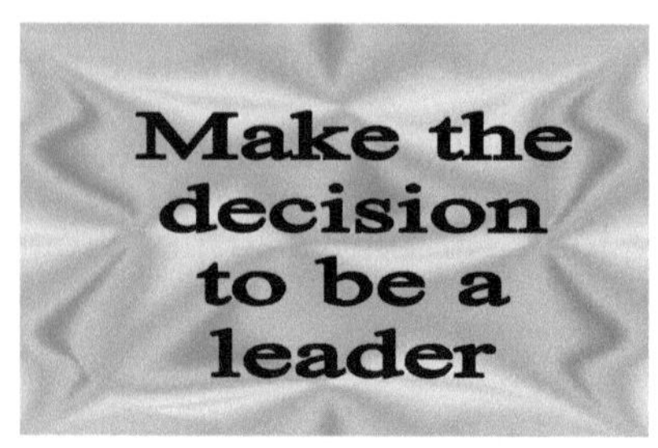

You make decisions in your life every day. You make choices all day, every moment. Followers tend to believe that it is easier to follow. They believe that it is easier to just allow others to dictate their lives to them. In some instances, they may be right, but there is a price to pay for followers. That price is life. You give up the deed to your life, you sell your birthright, when you decide to be a lifelong follower.

Leaders are inclined to believe that it is easier to lead and be the leader of their own life. They believe it is easier to govern their life than to risk putting it in the hands of unhealthy decision makers and negative planters. Leaders prefer to keep the deed to their life. All in all, decisions are constantly being made by every living being. Everyone has been given the gift of choice. Some individuals will choose to be followers and some individuals will choose to be leaders. Why follow when you can lead? After all, it is your life, you will ultimately and definitely be held accountable. You make choices everyday, why follow, when you can lead?

Fear! Fear prevents most people from leading. The fear of failure, of being insulted by peers, and of not belonging can immobilize any of us. The fear of the unknown keeps most people believing that it is easier to hand over their life and let someone more capable manage it. They lack self-esteem. These individuals have surpassed the low self-esteem phase they have no esteem. They do not believe they are capable of doing anything right. That is a lie. Climb up and out of that fear hole. Everyone is capable of doing many things right. Everyone can accomplish doing things right in their lives – everyone. That includes YOU!

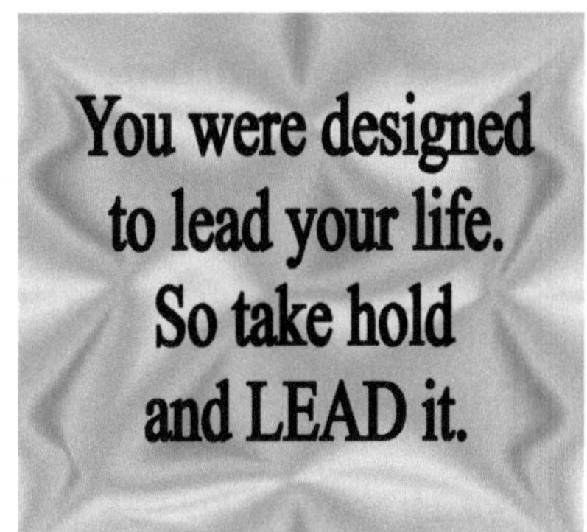

I charge you with leading. You are charged with taking hold of your life. You are charged with taking your life back from anyone you gave it up to – do it now. Take your life back and become the leader you were designed to be. Even with obstacles in your life, take control. Simply make the decision to be a leader. For some of you, at some point in your life, you were a leader, you were exhibiting leadership skills; you were actually running your show. For most of you, you are currently exhibiting your leadership skills and capabilities, but not in all areas of your life. No one was given a life, so that life could be handed over to someone else.

For all of you, you were designed to lead your life. You are charged with taking your life back. You must lead your life; you were created to do so. You are on the path to being an all encompassing leader. Say and know…

I have my own mind.

I was created to lead my own life.

I was not created to allow other people to have control over my life.

I have the deed to my own birthright.

I give myself permission to live my life.

I give myself permission to take my life out of the hands of negative influencers.

I give myself permission to be a leader.

I am not a follower. I never wanted to be a follower.

I know I am a leader. I have always known it.

I am already equipped with leadership abilities.

I have decided right now to be a leader in all major areas of my life.

I am a leader!

You are a leader! You were birthed to lead. You always had it in you. Now you have been given the seal of approval that you have your life back. Stamped approved - you are indeed a leader. Now that you know who you are, when it comes to follower and leaders there are more people you will need to address.

When you make a conscious decision to take charge of your life and you decide to become a leader, the first people you should stop following should be the negative planters in your life. They are toxic, poisonous, contaminated, and deadly. They are always waiting to strike their next victim. WARNING - at all cost you need to avoid these toxic people. Instead, surround yourself with positive planters.

Take out the old and bring in the new. Replacement is the key. Keep the old toxics from finding an opening into your thoughts. Choose positive planters for your life. Positive planters make great leaders. Positive planters are forever leading others in the right direction and they help to develop great leaders. Surround yourself with positive planters and strive to become a positive planter. This will equip you on your leadership path. Surround yourself with happy people who are striving to be successful. Attitudes are contagious and personalities rub off. Be in the company of people who want to see you succeed, encourage you to follow your dreams, inspire you to keep pressing on, cheer you on, believe in you, and sing your praises. Please know that these types of people have leadership personalities and they are leaders.

Because you desire to be a leader, start hanging around people who have a leader's personality. Start chilling with positive people. You will find that you will become that which you associate or aspire to be. If you want to follow someone, follow these positive leaders until you find yourself becoming a positive leader. Engage in the things that positive people engage in. In other words, do what positive people do. Say what positive leaders say. Watch and read what positive individuals watch and read. You will begin to think like a positive leader thinks, then guess what? You will become a positive leader.

Who You *Really* Are

At the beginning of the book you were asked who are you? You were placed on a soul searching journey. You probably thought you were all those negative things that the ignorant, sick, evil, and selfish people planted into your life. Many teens and young adults actually believed the negative hype. These young people actually started believing that they were predestined for failure. They bought into the forever told lie that they were not going to be successful, an asset to society, fruitful and prosperous. These misinformed young people actually believed that they were going to be nobodies, menaces to society, and unsuccessful.

No longer will you accept the negative. No longer will you allow your thoughts to tell you that you are not worthy and special. No longer will you believe the negative implants that the negative people planted in your garden of life. No longer will you be that low self-esteemed individual with a defeatist mentality. Die to that person.

Who You *Really* Are

Dreams are simply goals and aspirations already envisioned
DREAM BIG!!!
- ckendrick

Die to the ugly, confused, and unsure you. Awaken to the beautiful, focused, and determined new you. Awaken I say. Awaken to who you were originally designed to become. You are a beautiful and smart individual that are going to experience some great times in your life. Many people that attempted to destroy your life actually tried to keep you from seeing who you really are. Some negative minded people saw the greatness in you before your eyes were opened. They knew your destiny was bright. You are really destined for success.

So start thinking about all you ever wanted to become, think about all you wanted to achieve in your life, and then take it up a notch. At some point in your life, you were allowed to dream and you did just that – you dreamed. You fantasized. You saw a great future and you saw yourself in it. You envisioned your future. Do you remember Chasity who could not see past her present? At one point in her life she too had dreams. But for many young people their dreams were squashed, just like Chasity's dreams, due to people constantly trampling on them. Go ahead. Don't be afraid to dream. Dream! Dreams are simply achieved goals and aspirations already envisioned. So as you dream, you will start to bring about beautiful and great things in your life. Dream and dream some more. Dream and dream big. You must dream repeatedly and relentlessly. After all, practice does make you better. All professional race car drivers practiced. All professional baseball players dreamed and practiced. All professional singers and rappers had a desire, recognized that they had some talent, and they practiced. All doctors, airplane pilots, photographers, forensic scientists, lawyers, and professionals from all walks of life started with a dream. They did not allow anyone to take their dream and destiny from them. They each pursued their destiny. They all had to practice.

As I mentioned before, all things in life right now started with a thought. Someone took the time to think about how nice it would be if they could just sit instead of standing or sitting on the ground or floor. That individual invented the chair. Someone thought about how easier life would be if people could access water from within the house instead of going to a water-well to draw water. This person invented the indoor water system and faucet. Someone thought about how nice it would be to have cool water they invented the ice maker. Someone thought about how nice it would be if we could listen to music anywhere. Well you know how the story goes, tapes, CD's, mp3 players, ipods, etc. They started with a thought. They continued to dream. They birthed their thoughts to fruition. Their dreams became reality. All things are possible. If you can believe, you can achieve.

Right now the biggest challenge in your life is you. Your mindset and your frame of thinking will eventually close doors for you or open doors for you. When you change your frame of thinking, you change your destiny. When you know who you really are, then you

A positive mind equals a bright future - ckendrick

know that your future of success is simply waiting on you.

On becoming who you really are, the first step is to recognize what and who you consider yourself to be. For many people this reflection does not display positive results. When people reflect they are asking "Who am I?" "Who do I think I am?" "What do I consider myself to be?" Life's circumstances have taught the vast majority of people to focus on the negatives. We quickly remember the negative and unfortunate things that people have done. Also, we are more apt to focus on the negative things we have done. We often times allow those negative events to dictate our lives. But there are good things in you. You have done some really good and outstanding things in your life, for yourself, and for others.

When people reflect on who they really are the negative views may surfaces. You must filter out the negative views and thoughts about who you are. In order to do this you must have replacements. If people allow themselves to reflect long enough they will get past the negative mishaps and reflect right on into the positives that have occurred because of them.

Unfortunately, there are so many people who are afraid of listening to their inner man. These individuals are afraid of silence. You actually know the type of people I am referring to that are afraid of silence. These individuals will allow a television to play all night long. They say that they can not sleep unless the radio is playing. They are the ones that will blurt out in class if it is too quiet. They are the ones that will actually say, "It's to quiet in here, I've got to get out of here," and they literally leave the presence of silence. They are literally running from themselves. It is important that you take the time to reflect and hear what your inner man is saying. Some of these individuals actually run for a lifetime. Listening to your inner man helps to direct you. It tells you who you *really* think you are. So stop and listen.

The individuals that run from silence tend to hold themselves captive in a mental world of misery. These individuals often times become negative-minded people who physically grew up, but stayed a mental wreck. They don't allow themselves to grow up mentally. These are the self-enhanced negative garden planters who taught themselves to prey on others. They prey on and belittle others in hopes of making themselves feel better or important. They are miserable people, who want others to be miserable as well. Have you ever heard that misery loves company? Know that it is true.

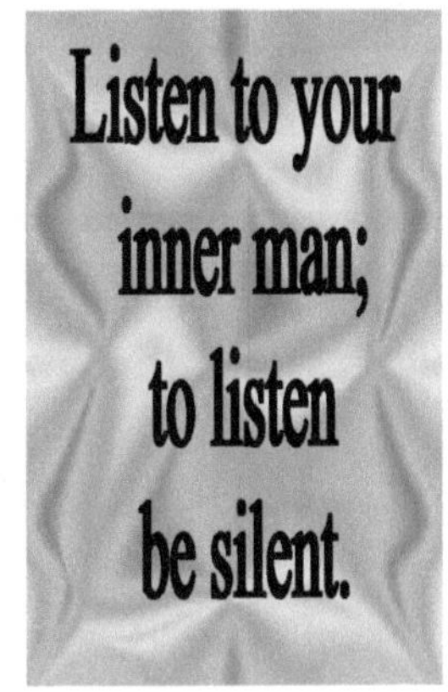

Nevertheless, you have to train yourself to endure the silence, listen to your inner man, and listen to your thoughts. Did you know that "listen" and "silent" consist of the same letters? I do not believe in coincidences. There is a reason why these two powerful words consist of the same letters. These words are related. They may be either siblings or first cousins. On a more serious note, "listen" and "silent" work hand in hand. In order to listen, you must be silent. When you are silent you are able to listen and hear. In your inner man world, is where you begin to heal and grow. You must be still and know that you will get through this first step – the sooner the better.

You have to think through the bad and ugly to get to the good. As you sift out the bad and ugly, your mental thought process will be left with only the good. You sift out, then you replace; you sift out, then you replace. It is a one to three ratio (1:3) process. So, for all the negative thoughts that surfaces you will recite a positive depiction of you three times. For example,

I do not like who I am. (1)

I love me! (1)

I **love** me! (2)

I love **me!** (3)

I have hurt so many people in my life (and you may have hurt some people in your life that you actually cared for).

I speak only good things about others.

I speak **only** good things about others.

I speak only **good** things about others.

I probably won't make it.

I am destined for greatness!

I am **destined** for greatness!

I am destined for **greatness**!

I don't think I will be successful.

I am a success!

I **am** a success!

I am a **success**!

I can't seem to get it right.

I **sow** good seeds and reap good things.

I sow **good** seeds and reap good things.

I sow good seeds and **reap** good things.

You must learn to speak those things that are not as though they already exist. You must constantly tell yourself powerful and great things. You have that ability. You are responsible for yourself. You are held accountable for your life. You have the power to bring your dreams into reality. Do it. Start practicing right now. Do not stop. Keep practicing, you are on your way to becoming great. You are on your way to becoming a professional. So, again I say, on becoming who you really are, the first step is to recognize what and who you consider yourself to be. You must practice, practice, practice, planting positive seeds in your garden of life.

On becoming who you really are, another step is to properly address your hurts and pains, and forgive those who hurt you and caused you pain. Of the two, the easiest is to address your hurts and pains. Addressing yourself should take place before addressing and forgiving others. When you are no longer emotional and hurting as much, you tend to be more clear-minded and forgiving.

We are often told to address our fears head on. If you have a fear of drowning get into the water; learn how to swim. We are to address our hurts and pains the same way, head on. As you reflect on your hurts and pains (not who wounded you, but your wounds), zoom in on how it actually alters your body. Some people become emotional and cry. Some people become angry and want to destroy the world. Some people heart rate increases. Their breathing changes to where they are sighing heavily or even panting as a precursor to hyperventilating. Some people, as they reflect on their wounds, their bodies will physically jerk. What I share with individuals, as they proceed through such a process, is to zoom in on how their bodies actually respond. Then techniques are put in place to address the body's reactions. These techniques are put in place to have responses serve as the replacements for reactions.

When the body reacts, it incorporates negative components as well. When the body responds, it feeds on positive fuel agents. So, when individuals are reflecting on life's scars, in an attempt to address them, their heart rate increases (reaction), then they are to start actively controlling their breathing (response). When anger (reaction) surfaces and individuals attempt to relieve themselves of such stress by engaging in a fight that is a reaction. More proper techniques to use are to go jogging, play basketball, hit a punching bag, or recite positive messages. These are responses. The point is – as you address your hurts and pains you are to respond rather than react.

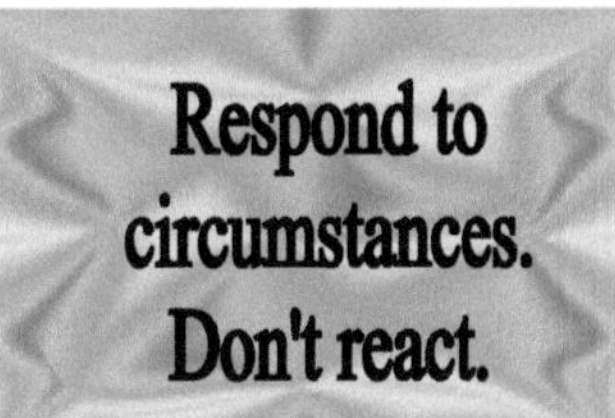

When the body is being presented with a medication, which hopefully will work to cure it of an illness, the doctor tests the patient by starting out with a prescribed dosage of the medication. Either the dosage will be suitable or it will need to be increased or decreased through trial and error. What helps the doctors to determine the proper dosage is the body of the patient. Therefore, follow up visits are scheduled. If the medication was well received by the body, it will be determined that the body <u>responded</u> well. If the medication was not well received by the body, it will be determined that the body had a negative <u>reaction</u> to the medication. To proceed the doctors then work on increasing or decreasing the dosage or will try another medication.

Work on teaching yourself how to respond rather than react. Utilizing techniques that will counter attack your thoughts will help when addressing your pains. When you feel changes in your body, you are to work on removing the reaction and replacing it with responses. Note that what is being address here are the hurts and pains that you have already encountered and have yet to address and let go. Yet, these same techniques can be used in future events.

The goal is to get you to address any mental hang ups you may have because of past misfortunes. Denounce those thoughts and feelings. They are in your past. Your present and future is what is important now. A wise person once said that she was going to place all her energies and investments on her future, because that is where she will be spending the rest of her life. From this point forward, as you reflect on your wounds acknowledge them for what they are – past wounds – nothing more, nothing less. Bandage them up, allow them to heal, remove the bandages, and move on. Have a funeral or toss them in the sea. Perform closure and move on. They are dead now. You are alive. Focus on your future.

Now the people that wounded you, the ones that caused you to cry in secret, and throw temper tantrums openly, address them. Some individuals tend to address and forgive the people that wounded them in person. Some individuals addressed and forgive others without having to speak with them. It is not as important as how you do it, what is most important is that you do it. Remember you are on a pathway to great success. You are walking into your full potential. You have established in the fact that you are on your way to inheriting great wealth and happiness. You refuse to remain incarcerated because of not forgiving.

It is your job to forgive. You are forgiving those who caused you strife in your life, not because they deserve it, but because you want to be free. You want to be free to come in contact with people that have done you wrong and you not become all bent out of shape. Meaning, you do not want to them to be able to alter your moment and day. When and if you ever see these people again, you should not want to experience an increase in your heart rate and a fluctuation in your breathing.

You are to forgive them, because you do not want to become a product of what they were hoping you will become; and that is to be an unsuccessful, miserable person. You have already taken your first steps toward walking into your life of happiness and impossibilities. Do not stop now. You have already learned why these people caused you pains and strife in your life in the previous chapters. You know the reasons varied as to why you experienced what you experienced in life with these negative gardeners. You should not want to allow them to send you into an attitude change from having a good day to having a bad day. Stop giving them that kind of power over your life. You are now given permission to be in control of your life. You will dictate the type of attitude you will display if and when you come in contact with these people. You are to forgive others so they will no longer have control over your life.

People tend to gain control over others lives only when the others allow them to gain the control. Individuals give up control of their lives when they allow the presence or actions of others to cause them to act out, become angry, fight, curse, and even destroy. When others tempt you, they are hoping that you lose control, lose your cool, or act out in a manner that will cause you to reap negative repercussions.

Take for instance; Brian is having a problem with Chase. Brian secretly and craftily teases and taunts Chase in the school cafeteria and then in class. Brian knew when to time his actions so he will not be seen as an instigator in front of authority figures. Chase finally becomes frustrated and angry. His emotions take over, which leads to him not even caring who is present. He loses his composure and begins to openly yell at Brian. As the moments pass, the verbal outburst turns into him approaching Brian, them pushing or hitting Brian. They are both sent to the authorities. Brian is released and returns to class, because he chose not to retaliate. Chase is suspended and still yelling, "It's not fair, and it ain't over."

Well what took place is that Brian was the one who had a problem with Chase. Brian wanted Chase to lose control and get in trouble. Brian was successful in making life a little miserable for Chase. Brian was successful with taking control of Chase's life. He wanted something to happen to Chase, and with the help of Chase he accomplished his goal. Brian played Chase on strings like a puppet.

On the other hand, Chase gave Brian control of his life, when he allowed Brian to change his attitude. Chase relinquished control of his life to Brian, when he chose to react rather than respond. Chase reacted when he became angry and when he pushed Brian. Chase could have responded in the same situation by not allowing himself to become angry and by telling school officials and his parents. Chase mentally angered himself into a state that caused him to overstep the rights of another individual. Chase was bound, and held in captivity by Brain's actions. Chase simply surrendered his freedom to Brian's mean acts. Brian's mission was accomplished.

If you ever find yourself in a similar predicament where someone is trying to play you like a puppet, you need to know that you have all the power. You were not made to be a puppet. You need to properly handle the situation without getting yourself into a sticky situation. Do not give up your power. Do not fall prey to someone who is on a mission to destroy you. Simply, stay cool and level headed, do not react, but respond only if you must. Then quickly remove yourself from the situation. You have won. You leave still with the power and the control.

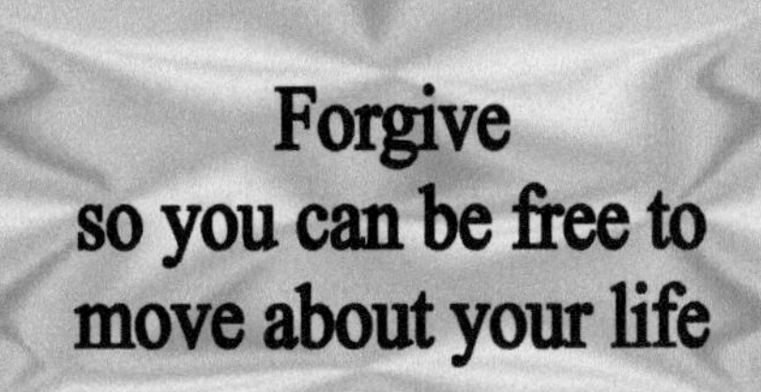

Nevertheless, you have a decision to make. Do you want to be free or do you want to be bound? Do you want to have total control of your life or do you want others to be your control pilot. You have the power to control your destiny. You are equipped with everything you need in order to overcome a non-forgiving attitude. So go get your life back. You will no longer be bound by someone who caused you to have to deal with unnecessary and undeserving struggles in your life. But you made it through. Since you were tough enough to actually make it through the actual events, you are definitely tough enough to make it through changing your mindset. It is a choice. All you have to do is decide to forgive. Just like we can decide to hold a grudge we can decide to forgive. Just like we can decide to pay others back for the wrongs they do against you, we can forgive them. Decisions are simply being made. Now decide to forgive so you can be free to move about your life.

You can place your focus on a great investment, your future. How you handle your life can be the greatest investment you can ever make. Invest wisely. Don't allow not being able to forgive block you from such a great investment. To proceed to your path ahead, you must address and take the path within. Check yourself and determine this day to let go of the painful past.

If you need to, practice forgiving in order to get past this step. If practice is going to help set you free then do what you have to do; even if it's reciting I forgive you Kelly. I forgive you Mike. I forgive you daddy. I forgive you Mr. Perry. Listed are some practicing tips. Work on freeing yourself by forgiving. Work on forgiving everyone. Insert names and whatever you need to insert into the sentences. Do it as often as you need to, because you are going to be set free today. There will be no more chains on your mind keeping you from walking happily into your destiny of blessings.

I forgive you, ______________

I hold no hard feelings towards you, __________

Today, _(today's date)_ I am making a conscious decision to free myself. I know _(person's name)_ has done some mean and thoughtless things to me like, _(past event)_, _(past event)_, and _(past event)_. I know I did not deserve these unkind words and acts. Those words and acts will no longer hold me in mental bondage. I denounce those deadly obstacles. I am now forgiving _(person's name)_ for planting bad seeds in my garden of life. I, _(your name)_ refuse to believe the mean and belittling comments that were spoken over my life. I, refuse to be held in misery because of your callous act(s). I am a new person. I have a renewed mind. I am alive. I am free. I am in control of my life. I, _(your name)_ am destined for greatness!

Know that you are set free. Know that great days are awaiting you. Tell yourself "Great days are awaiting me!" What you have done is you have taken your focus and energies off the past and the people that caused you to suffer. Instead you have placed your focus on you and who you really are.

Now that you have 1) listened to your inner man on who you are, 2) filtered out the negative portrayals of who you are and replaced them with positive images, and 3) addressed and forgiven your hurts and pains, you can begin to work on being more active with bridging your thoughts with your future. This is different from sifting out the negative ideology that was placed in your life about who you were. The focus here is more on imparting in you who you really are, who you were born to be, the person you once knew before all chaos broke out in your life. The focal point here is now working towards achieving your dreams and being successful, an asset, fruitful, and prosperous. Turn back to your original state, the person who you were born to be. Remember you are of your Father, and he is all positive and good.

Nothing is impossible, if you believe you can move mountains, then you will move mountains. You move mountains by moving pebbles, rocks, and boulders. Work is involved. The problems that most people have encountered in life, that left them hopeless, were that they had faith that one day their situations will improve and for some reason they did not improve. Still, I am a firm believer that their life will improve, if they work at it or practice some. Faith without works produces nothing. That is the truth. Some people had the faith yet lived a lifetime in their mental jail cells, and they simply left out the work part. We have to work some. I am telling you –there is a responsibility part that we all have to face.

Working on perfecting a positive mental attitude of who you really are is definitely necessary. Because life tends to throw curve balls from time to time, you must be ready to adjust your swing. In order to be prepared you should stay ahead of the game. Practice for life's test. Do not wait for the test to be placed in front of you, and then you attempt to determine what to do.

When instructors tell their students that a test will be given on Friday, or at the end of the term, or after the review of the entire chapter, they in essence are telling students to study and be prepared to be tested. It is the students' responsibility to prepare for the test prior to the test being issued, if they want to do well on the test. Life's tests are similar; if you prepare for them you tend to do better when they are placed before you. So equip yourself. You equip yourself by taking on a positive attitude and an optimistic outlook on life. You equip yourself by embracing a positive approach to life. You equip yourself by saying and knowing who you really are.

As I near the conclusion of this chapter and book I will like to leave you with riches that have the power to enrich, develop, and change your life forever. I can only bring life to you; it is up to you to embrace it. I, along with many more people, love you and want you to reach your proper destination. It is up to you to make the ultimate decision. Your life is in your hands. You hold the key to your doors of opportunity. Be smart. Love yourself. By all means, handle your life with care.

Recite as often as possible the following comments.

I am a new person.

I am destined to be great.

I have power invested in me.

I am in charge of my destiny.

I am love and I am loved.

I am a beautiful person.

I am beautiful within.

I am a gift.

I am alive.

I am righteous.

I am determined.

I am built to endure.

I have a sound mind.

I am walking in faith.

I am being transformed.

I am safe and protected.

I am destined for success.

I am a good investment.

I am in control.

I am necessary.

I am a forgiver.

I am from my Father's great genes.

I am an original and not a copy.

I have a bright future that awaits me.

I am forgiven.

I am capable.

I am blessed.

I am healthy.

I am valuable.

I reap reward.

I BELIEVE, THEREFORE I AM.

My Love this is who you really are – and then some! I pray peace and blessings over your life.

Sow Good Seeds

Reap Great Rewards

Words to Remember

Who you believe and say you are is what you'll always be. Perception is everything. How you view your life is up to you.

Page 11

I wish more of you knew your worth, because then you would not have to wear your bling-bling around your neck or in your ears to measure your worth. Your bling-bling is all over you and all in you.

Page 17

Although you cannot change the past, one of your responsibilities is to learn from your past. The bad and ugly experiences, vow to not repeat them in your life when you are able to start making adult decisions. Make those bad and ugly events a foot stool for you to climb as you reach your destiny. The good experiences take hold of them, cherish them, and when you repeat them make sure you add extra seasoning.

Page 19

You are the gardener and you hold the gardening tools to your life. You will determine how things will be planted in your life. You will determine how the upkeep of your garden will look. Take care of your garden.

Page 25

You can change your world one thought at a time. It is up to you to really determine what kind of world you want to have and live in for the rest of your life.

Page 30

Your life is in your hands. Fragile – handle with care.

Words to Remember

You are empowered. You were given the power to choose. You have dominion over your attitude. You are the gardener in your garden.

Page 34

When you open your hand to let go of the past, that same hand is open to receive your future. When you become open to letting go, the future will rush into your life.

Page 38

Please believe that a healthy mindset is a positive mind that is constantly being feed positive thoughts. Positive outcomes are direct results of positive thoughts and actions. That which you believe today will surely affect that which you achieve tomorrow.

Page 50

Open up to life. Allow your life to be a thoroughfare for reward to freely flow in and out of it. Take the limits off.

Page 51

You will have all your needs met. Do your part. Take ownership of your life. Do what is right. Be positive. Speak positive words to yourself. Feed yourself. Feed others.

Page 52

Everyone has been given the gift of choice. Some individuals will choose to be followers and some individuals will choose to be leaders. Why follow when you can lead?

Page 60

Words to Remember

You are a leader. You were birthed to lead. You always had it in you.

Page 62

Surround yourself with positive planters and strive to become a positive planter. Surround yourself with happy people who are striving to be successful.
Attitudes are contagious and personalities rub off.

Page 63

Right now the biggest challenge in your life is you. Your mindset and your frame of thinking will eventually close doors for you or open doors for you. When you change your frame of thinking, you change your destiny.

Page 67

You are to forgive others so they will no longer have control over your life.

Page 75

Forgive. Like you choose to hold a grudge, you can choose to forgive. Like you choose to pay others back for their mistreatment of you, you can choose to forgive them.

Page 78

Because life tends to throw curve balls from time to time, you must be ready to adjust your swing.

Page 81

Your life is in your hands. Fragile – handle with care.

Your Life is in Your Hands

FRAGILE

Handle with Care

ABOUT THE AUTHOR

C. Lisa Kendrick is the founder and LEAD facilitator of L.E.A.D. Training Solutions. She conducts workshops, seminars, and speaking engagements. She shares her messages on attitude, motivation, and success with not only youths, but also parents and adults that impact the lives of teenagers. She is devoted to enriching and developing people, one person or one team at a time.

Lisa is a certified Life Coach, a certified Global Career Development Facilitator, and a certified Workforce Development Professional. She is a personal empowerment advocate. She attended the University of Georgia and Walden University. She is an advocate for instilling and bringing forth dreams in people. Her mission is to inform all people of the greatness that is in them and their rights to their destiny and full potential. She is currently working on another book.

For more information or to schedule C. Lisa Kendrick for a speaking engagement visit www.leadtrainingsolutions.com

To order additional copies

ONLINE www.lulu.com www.amazon.com

EMAIL ckendrick12@gmail.com or clk@leadtrainingsolutions.com

www.ingramcontent.com/pod-product-compliance
Ingram Content Group UK Ltd.
Pitfield, Milton Keynes, MK11 3LW, UK
UKHW041925190726
13854UKWH00003B/1443

9 780615 162126